INTRODUCTION

This book is devoted to the area of Sheffield loosely described as the City Centre. I have allowed myself a bit of licence in choosing the photographs but all of them were taken by myself.

To the south the extent is to London Road and Bramall Lane. Northwards I have gone as far as West Bar and to the west no farther than Division Street. Eastwards I have included the Wicker Arches. That roughly defines my area.

I believe that this city has changed more during my lifetime than at any period in its history. It is destined to change even more if the many plans now mooted are to become a reality. Those of my age will have their opinions as to how it is a better and how it is a worse city than it was. I will not bore you with mine. The majority of people who buy this book will live with the changes long after I am gone. I sincerely hope that they are in for a glorious future.

One new feature in this, the third of my "Camera" series is the introduction of an index. From my own experience I find it frustrating when seeking a particular picture from a book to have to thumb through the entire contents to find it. So in this instance I have sacrificed one of my eighty pages to provide an index.

I have chosen an alphabetic arrangement by streets as being as logical as any other. Beginning with Angel Street and ending with The Wicker the arrangement is A to Z with a few exceptions where two upright photographs are paired on a single page. The other exception is the colour section occupying the eight centre pages.

INDEX

This is Angel Street with Water Lane to the right and Snig Hill to the left. This was the site that was to be developed to build the new police station and magistrates' court. The tall building lacking its roof was Duncan Gilmour's brewery. Hidden behind the Direct Curtains building was Water Lane police station. The date of the photograph was 18th August 1965. Notice how the single tram track had survived five years after all tramcars had gone.

Angel Street. The Canon Cinema, 13th May 1987. Formerly the ABC Cinema. This whole area has been redeveloped.

A rather dismal view taken from the back of the GPO around 1968 looking down the road that is known as Baker's Hill.
All these buildings would be swept away a few years later.

The Philharmonic concerts have been held in the City Hall since its opening in 1932. The Gaumont cinema is showing the 1973 film "The Stone Killers".

Barker's Pool after the Gaumont cinema had been demolished and the foundations for the red girder building were being laid. The date is the 29th of April 1986.

This beast paid a visit to Sheffield in 1977 - possibly to celebrate the Queen's Jubilee. I don't know who had the

Blonk Street on Wednesday the 18th August 1965. Apart from the few shops this part of Blonk Street belonged mainly to Samuel Osborne's. All the visible buildings have now gone.

Blonk Street taken on the same day as the previous photograph but this time showing the opposite side of the street. Davison's have gone but some of the other buildings are still standing at the time of writing. Allison's carpets occupied one of these buildings. Mr. Allison set up his carpet business here. There must be many who still walk on his carpets.

Bramall Lane, Saturday 4th August 1973. The final cricket match that ended 118 years of cricket at the Lane. W.G. Grace, Ranji, Hobbs, Bradman and many other legendary names have trodden this hallowed turf in those 118 years. This particular Roses match ended in a draw. The Yorkshire team on that day was: Boycott, Lumb, Sharpe, Hampshire, Johnson, Old, Bairstow, Carrick, Cooper, Nicholson and Bore.

Bridge Street bus station in July 1974 looking towards Bridge Street on the right and Spring Street on the left. The Law Courts now occupy the left of the picture and at the time of writing the whole area is undergoing re-development.

Cambridge Street 1972. The Barleycorn was an older inn than its modernist facade would suggest.
It dates back to a time when the street was known as Coalpit Lane

Change Alley in 1965
shortly before it
disappeared for ever.

In 1973 small shops such as this could survive in the very centre of Sheffield. This tobacconist was to be found at No. 27 Division St. The date is the 9th November 1973.

Church Street around 1977 with the underpass that led across High Street and Fargate to Boots, the Chemist. Note the different liveries of the two buses - one South Yorkshire and the other Sheffield

Dixon Lane before the street sellers were told to leave. The date was 1972.

Castle Square on 16th October 1960. Much of the devastation caused by the Blitz of 1940 is still evident but would not be so for much longer. Two days before this photo was taken the last tram had passed this point and the new car line was still being

Change Alley is there on 14th August 1965 but only just, All the buildings had gone but motor cars could still gain access. The road connected High Street to Norfolk Street.

Traffic control in 1960 was in the hands of policemen. This one had his own platform for controlling traffic from Church Street, High Street and Fargate.

Eyre Lane at Howard Street. The shop, No. 15 Howard Street was Clough Ibbotson's. They sold typewriters before computer printers came on the scene. On the right of the photo can be seen the City Library. All this area has gone. The date of the photograph is 14th August 1965.

An assortment of vintage cars are here seen parked on newly cleared land above Eyre Street on 14th August 1965. I can spot a Ford Popular and a Morris Minor Traveller, possibly also a Triumph Herald but there my knowledge ceases.

Fargate 1975

Here is Arnold "Gerry" Taylor - the flower seller with a past. His story created much interest when featured in the Star along with this photo. He fought in WW1 but thereafter scratched a living by selling scrap, dying flowers and whatever else he could lay his hands on.

This Fiesta poster of 1974 in Fargate displays an impressive list of star attractions. Ella Fitzgerald - 'nuff said; Mike Reid came up via "The Comedians"; The Grumbleweeds had their day. About Gene Pitney and the Bee Gees you will need to consult someone younger than I.

Left: a corner of Fitzalan Square as it was in 1973. The Classic Cinema and Barclay's Bank have both gone. The Bell pub has now closed. Peter Cushing was to be seen in "Dracula AD" at the cinema. This was a horror film from Hammer Studios.

Above: The Empire Hotel pub stood at the corner of Eyre Street and Charles Street. Its site now lies under Arundel Gate. The date is 1965.

The Classic Cinema in Fitzalan Square as it was in 1977. The cinema finally closed in 1982.

There are not many photographs around of the Odean Cinema when it was still showing films.
Here the 1967 film "Thoroughly Modern Millie" is being shown. The Elephant pub. on the corner of Norfolk Street is also prominent. The date is 1968.

This is George Street in1974. It's facade is not very different now but this photograph was taken when it was still a bank and its interior little changed from Victorian times. Over the doorway can be seen "Sheffield Banking Company". This company was formed in 1831 taking over "George's Coffee House". Over the years the premises were extended and improved. A nice feature of this photograph is to see a gentleman - presumably the manager - opening up the premises. At the time of the photograph the Westminster Bank was in occupation. A fine photograph of the interior in its heyday is to be seen at page 26 of R.E. Leader's "The Sheffield Banking Company Limited" 1916.

A view up Fitzwilliam St. from The Moor to West Street as it was in 1977.
Much new development has taken place along this road.

Boots corner where Fargate meets High Street on a rainy day in 1969 shortly after the new underpass had been built so that pedestrians could get across what were then two busy roads.

This band is leading the Lord Mayor's parade past the Hole in the Road for the Queen's Silver Jubilee in 1977.

This is a panoramic view of the Castle Square underpass, more commonly known as The Hole in the Road. It was built in 1965, opened in 1967 and closed in 1994 so that the new Supertram could pass over it. Entrances were on High Street (east and west), Angel Street and Arundel Gate. It became a popular thoroughfare with its own underground shops and even an aquarium of tropical fish. This photograph dates from around 1975. It was taken with a Russian panoramic camera that I owned at the time.

Not everyone was quite so enthusiastic about the Silver Jubilee of 1977. Certainly these sellers of the "Socialist Worker" were not.

Saturday, 8th October 1960 and the building of the new Sheffield Polytechnic is under way in Howard Street. It would be a long time before it became Hallam University.

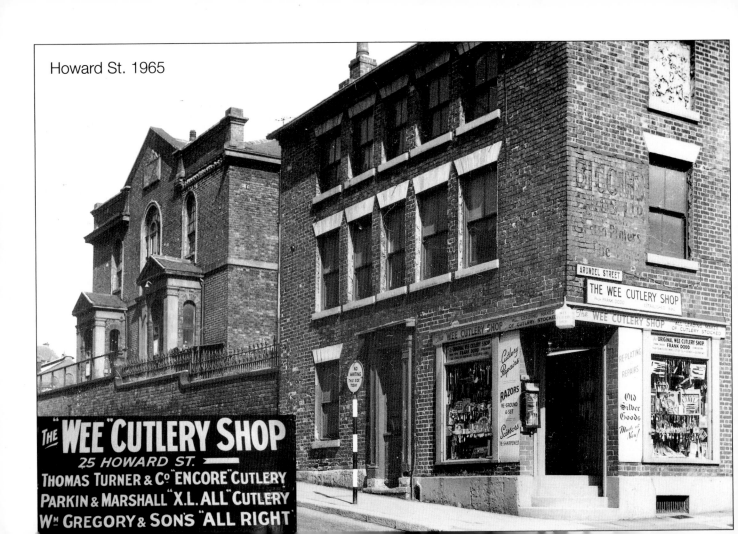

Howard St. 1965

"THE "WEE" CUTLERY SHOP
25 HOWARD ST.
THOMAS TURNER & Co "ENCORE" CUTLERY
PARKIN & MARSHALL "X.L. ALL" CUTLERY
Wᵐ GREGORY & SONS "ALL RIGHT"

Norfolk Street in 1965 when big changes were afoot. The Lyceum can be seen but the Crucible theatre was still a pipe-dream.

This is 1960 - before the hole-in-the-road and just after the last of the old trams had passed. In the distance is the old bank and cinema. The policeman on points duty is a sight now almost unseen. There are still a few pedestrian crossings left but not in the city centre. They were created by Leslie Hore-Belisha, then Minister of Transport, in 1934 and the orange globes were forever known as "Belisha beacons". Note the two "Keep Left" signs - one of the old-fashioned type and the other more modern.

Before pedestrianisation The Moor was a popular place for shopping as the crowds in this view taken in 1974 show.

Buses on The Moor before pedestrianisation (horrible word but I don't know of another!). The date is 1974.

This ia a view of Moorfoot in 1977 before the Manpower Services building was built completely blocking off The Moor - an ancient highway. It shows the roundabout at the bottom of Ecclesall Road with a view up London Road. The Lansdowne Night Club on the upper left stands out.

Another view of the bottom of the Moor shows Ecclesall Road with the much-loved Sheffield & Ecclesall Co-operative Store, rather dwarfed by the high-rise flats. The date is 1977.

One of the saddest acts of the Royal Mail has been the closure of the Head Post Office in Fitzalan Square - a superb edifice purpose built in a classic style both inside and out. Now customers have to queue inside a department store. As if in shame the old red phone boxes have slunk away.

The old Lyceum nearing the end of its life with a Christmas pantomime.
The date is 1967. It had a period as a bingo hall before the magnificent restoration of the 1990s.

Tudor Square.
The Lyceum
Theatre after
restoration.

The Sheaf
Market in 1967
with the Market
bobby in the
foreground.

A nighttime photo of the Gaumont cinema. The film "The French Lieutenant's Woman" dates from 1981. At this time the cinema had just a few more years life before it

In 1977 the new Town Hall extensions were not quite complete. Notice that in this picture they are still fenced off.

The Egg Box shortly before its demolition. The date is 26th August 2001, viewed from Arundel Gate.
I was as glad as everyone else to see it go but now I am not so sure. It had a certain grandeur

In its continuing efforts to improve city transport the Council, in the 1980s, introduced horse buses.

They proved quite popular with everyone except the horses.

Above:
The Royal George on Carver Street will be known to all who saw the Playhouse production of "The Stirrings at Sheffield" which largely centred on William Broadbent, the landlord.

Left:
Norfolk Street in 1965. The old Sheffield firm of Pawson and Brailsford can be seen and lower down can just be seen the Sheffield Club.

Left is Norfolk Street as it was in 1960. Prominent are Wilks ironmongers and the Victoria Hall.

London Road 1974. No wonder it was difficult to get into Allister McTaggart's waiting room. He was one of the best vets in Sheffield - and the cheapest.

This was Norfolk Row before pedestrianisation. The year is 1967 and the YMCA is up for sale. Sheffield Photo Company is the shop past the archway.

When bulldozers moved in to clear the Grand Hotel in 1974, coupled with sadness at the loss of a fine hotel was a sudden opportunity to photograph the whole of the south side of the Central School. Previously it had been impossible to get a view of the whole facade and following the redevopment of the site it has once again become impossible. I took two photographs and by a miracle of modern technology it has been possible to stitch them together to obtain what is probably a unique photograph. The school went through a number of changes after it was built in 1887. At first it was a council school. It then became the Pupil Teachers' Centre. Latterly it was the Central Secondary School and the Central Grammar School. Since then it has lain empty while vast sums have been spent building new chip board and breeze block replacements.

A view from Park Hill taken in 1975. In the foreground is the Midland Railway but filling the whole of the centre is Rodger's massive works above Sheaf Street.

In 1973 excavations were under way for the building of an extension to the Town Hall. The modernistic design was to be disrespectfully known as "The Egg Box". Its life was to be no more than twenty-five years.

These tram shelters on Pinstone Street were removed in 1985. They were fixed to the wall that had originally marked the edge of St. Paul's churchyard before that buiding was demolished in 1938. From that date they bordered the gardens that were officially St. Paul's Gardens but commonly known as The Peace Gardens. Possibly because they were no longer felt to be safe they were dismantled and another much-loved landmark disappeared.

To see passengers climbing aboard a tram was a common enough sight until Saturday October 8th 1960. That day was the the last time it would happen and also the date of this photograph. The steps were quite a challenge to elderly folk as can clearly be seen.

A wet day on Pinstone Street at St. Paul's Parade before work began on the new Peace Gardens in 1973. Notice that the rain could not deter the Salvation Army collector.

The Queen's Head on Pond Hill in the days before the Rodgers' industrial buildings had been demolished. The old pub is one of Sheffield's most photographed buildings but this background seldom appears. The date is 1977.

Pond Street bus station in 1965 before it became The Interchange. Set out like an angel cake we have the buses, then Rodgers' works and above it all Park Hill flats.

Here Pond Street and Flat Street meet with Pond Hill beyond. Visible on Pond Hill at No. 19 is the Lyceum - an eighteenth century hotel and public house also known as the Horse and Jockey, now long since gone. The date of the photograph is 14th August 1965.

The River Don viewed from Blonk Street bridge on 12th January 1974 showing the extensions to Osborn's works supported on stilts to make the most of available space. To the right can be seen the Royal Victoria Hotel - now the Holiday Inn.

Rockingham Street in 1965 viewed from Wellington Street with the Rockingham Arms pub to the left. The old car parking post will be remembered by older motorists.

Sheaf Square taken on 27th December 1976. There is a good view of Davy's foods building. The block of buildings on the south side of Howard Street were all demolished.

Snig Hill 1973

I, personally, reckon this the best bit of sculpture that ever adorned a Sheffield street.
It represents the Black Swan pub or "the mucky duck".

Tenter Street at White Croft showing Granville Works, now demolished.
April 1977.

A view down Townhead Street towards the Playhouse Theatre and the Methodist Sunday School. On the right are the Townhead flats - Sheffield's first attempt at municipal housing and still in use. The date is 1970.

The corner shop here is not the Art Shop but Jenkinson & Marshall's stationer's shop. It was located at the corner of Surrey Street and Tudor Street. Mr. Bob Marshall presided over it in its later days. He was a charming man of the old school. The Council owned the property and when they gave him notice to quit he was devastated. He relocated at the corner of Carver Street and West Street. Everything in the picture was demolished to create Tudor Square. The lady is passing an alleyway that led to the backs of the houses on Surrey Street. I am told that at one time coaching horses were stabled up this

Tudor Square.
A view of the Lyceum before its restoration. The car park area is now grassed down.
The date is around 1979.

Tudor Square as it was in 1968. Towards the left is the old Nether chapel - now replaced. The buildings to the right formed Tudor Way. The cars are parked on the site of the old Theatre Royal that was burnt down before the war. The tall building was in use by Wilks the ironmongers. Pretty well everything on this photograph has now been demolished.

Tudor Way viewed from the roof of Hay's building - don't ask me how I got there. The Adelphi Hotel to the right was one of Sheffield's most historic pubs. It was here that the Yorkshire Cricket Club was formed in 1863 and four years later in 1867 Sheffield Wednesday F.C. was founded. It narrowly escaped the flames when the Theatre Royal burned down but it could not escape the bulldozer. The Crucible Theatre now stands on the site. Photographed in 1968.

Tudor Square as it was in 1975. The Lyceum was reduced to advertising the new Crucible Theatre both of which can be seen here. The road led from Norfolk Street to Surrey Street.

Union Street in 1969 towards Charles Street at a time when Brook Shaw's motors occupied the corner site. The other buildings faced the Empire theatre and shortly after it went, they went.

The Sheffield Picture Palace cinema on Union Street was the first purpose-built cinema in Sheffield. It opened in 1910 and was demolished in 1964. The film displayed "The King and I" was the last to be shown there. It was always known as "The Palace, Union Street".

West Street 1970. The Saddle pub has now been replaced with a modern building. It served beer throughout the nineteenth and most of the twentieth century.

Victoria Station steps formed a useful shortcut between the station and the Wicker Arches. It may have been a little daunting for holiday makers with heavy suitcases but before the welfare state there was always an unemployed chap willing to carry them up the steps for you for sixpence.

On the other hand many buses and trams stopped near the steps. The alternative was to walk down the Wicker, on Blonk Street and up the Station approach.

This photograph was taken in 1984 after the station was closed but before these steps had been sealed off. Surely they are an important piece of industrial archaeology and would even now make a pleasant shortcut to the markets.
Possibly the Holiday Inn owners would not welcome such a move.

This is Water Lane looking up towards Snig Hill. The building on the left was Duncan Gilmour's brewery - nearing the end of its life. This area is now part of the new police station and magistrates' court.

Water Lane leading down to Bridge Street. The large building was the the Bridge Inn - an old pub. previously called the Bridge Tavern. For an interesting account of it see Michael Liversidge's book "An A to Z of Sheffield Public Houses" if you can find a copy.

This corner building was Nos. 94-96 West Bar. At one time it was the George and Dragon public house and also an early music hall. Ignore the ground floor and look above to see an imposing building - suitable for Victorian night life. It disappeared after Ellis Pearson - glass merchants - vacated the premises in the 1970s.

The Wicker in 1965.
The Big Gun public house dates from the 1790s. It seems that the landlord is in conversation with a passer-by. Across the road are the offices of Samuel Osborne. They monopolised the whole of this part of Sheffield as far as the Victoria Station Approach.

Photographs of the Wicker Arches are almost always taken from the other side.
This view from Spital Hill shows those buildings that were demolished to allow the Parkway feeder road to be built.
There is the Wicker Cinema, latterly known as Studio 7, and between that and the Westminster Bank were
Nos. 108 (a confectioners); 114 (a cafe); 116 (a tobacconist); 118 (a dry cleaner); 120 (A newsagent);
122 (house furnishings).
The photograph dates from the early 1970s.